HOPE BEYOND DESPAIR

Finding TRUTH after a Loved One's Suicide

JULIE GOSSACK

Hope Beyond Despair
Finding TRUTH after a Loved One's Suicide

ISBN: 978-1-936141-42-5

Cover Design by Amelia Schussman

Printed in the United States of America

Focus Publishing
PO Box 665
Bemidji, Minnesota 56619

TABLE OF CONTENTS

ENDORSEMENTS

The little booklet you hold in your hand is one of the best resources you will ever find on the topic of suicide. I say that without reservation. I am a pastor and, sadly, I've walked with many people through the heart-wrenching experience of having a friend or family member commit suicide. Julie has been there too, as you will see when you read her words. Her insights are personal, thoroughly biblical, and filled with compassion. It is easy to believe that there is no way to find comfort for yourself or give someone else comfort when the pain is caused by suicide. However, the truths contained in this booklet, if embraced, can comfort the soul. Nothing can completely erase the pain, but truth can sustain you to walk through it in a God-honoring, Christ-exalting way. I commend this booklet to you wholeheartedly.

> **Dr. Bryan Hughes**, Senior Pastor, Grace Bible Church, Bozeman, MT. Author of *8:28: Unlocking God's Promise*, and *Jesus's Teaching on the Last Days: Understanding the Olivet Discourse in Matthew 24-25.*

We live in a culture that frequently glorifies suicide, but there is nothing glorious about it. Suicide is one of the most destructive sins imaginable. It is clearly destructive to the one who commits suicide, bringing an end to this life, but the destructive wake of pain and anguish for the loved ones left behind is overwhelming. Suicide has hit our own congregation hard within the last few years. The pain is unbelievable. It is hard to talk about. For these reasons, and more, I am thankful for Julie Gossack's book, *Hope Beyond Despair*. Julie speaks from firsthand experience. The question is where can we possibly find hope after the suicide of a loved one? How can we sort through the lies and the truth? Julie rightly points us to hope in Christ and His sufficient Word. I trust that this resource will be widely used to help many people discover or rediscover the comforts of a loving Father through His Word.

Dr. Brian Borgman, Pastor of Grace Community Church in Minden, NV. Author of *Feelings and Faith: Cultivating Godly Emotions in the Christian Life* (Crossway).

Grieving death from suicide means experiencing and working through unspeakable pain and confusion. From her personal journey, Julie understands this anguish and addresses it with biblical clarity and wise counsel. In this booklet, you will discover the way forward following the tragedy of suicide. *Hope Beyond Despair* leads the hurting survivor to the only source of true help: the God of all comfort. I highly recommend it for anyone whose life has been touched by this trial.

Pamela Gannon, RN, MABC, ACBC Certified Biblical Counselor, Grace Bible Church in Bozeman, MT. Adjunct Professor of Biblical Counseling, Montana Bible College. Co-author *In the Aftermath: Past the Pain of Childhood Sexual Abuse.*

Hope Beyond Despair is very well written, theologically sound, practical, very relational and highly credible, given Julie Gossack's roster of sad 'credentials' in dealing with suicide. Few could speak with Julie's experiential authority on this subject and her "lies/truth" scheme is, in my opinion, down to brass tacks on both ends. Julie faces the hard questions without flinching, because she has had to face them herself, and in this booklet she provides the right biblical answers if faith is there to greet them. I will certainly use this booklet as a resource for our people and would think any sound, Bible-believing Christian leader would also.

Jim Andrews, Senior Pastor, Lake Bible Church, Oswego, OR. Radio host of The Final Word**.** Author, *Polishing God's Monuments: Pillars of Hope for Punishing Times* (Shepherd Press), *Marriage without Remorse: Rules for the Road* (Truth Encounters).

INTRODUCTION

Disbelief. Horror. Gut-wrenching shock. Trying to make sense of the senseless. There are no answers. Only pain. Loss. Emptiness. Devastation.

Giant Despair has triumphed again! His dark dungeon has claimed yet another. His whispered counsel, "Do away with your life," was heeded. And it's your loved one who succumbed to his treachery.

There is no heartache equal to that of losing a friend or family member to suicide. Wading through the wreckage and debris is confusing and agonizing. Yet, there is help. There is hope. This help and hope is found only in Jesus Christ. There may be programs and clinics that offer surface-level assistance and temporary comfort, but true help, true hope is found only in Jesus. He alone gives genuine comfort to your inward being. He alone gives healing to your heart. Only Christ can replace anguish and hopelessness with transcendent peace and enduring joy.

Hope Beyond Despair will bring solace and relief to your emptiness and confusion. This booklet provides a personal and honest perspective of grieving a suicide. It weaves the truth of Scripture and the hope of the Gospel with the author's candid experience to help answer questions and concerns as you grieve your loved one's suicide.

CHAPTER ONE
DOUBTING CASTLE

John Bunyan's classic allegory, *The Pilgrim's Progress*, portrays a fictional character that is all too real for many: the wicked Giant Despair. This colossal fiend seizes pilgrims who wander near Doubting Castle. He secures them in his dark, stinking dungeon where they never see the light of day. This mighty hulk insults, ridicules, and beats his victims regularly and without mercy. They are left to lament bitterly in the recesses of the black and gloomy chamber. Each day the Giant reappears, breathing threats and advising the pilgrims to do away with themselves. "Drink this poison," he snarls, "for why should you choose life seeing it is attended with so much bitterness?"[1]

"Drink this poison," he snarls, "for why should you choose life seeing it is attended with so much bitterness?"

Bunyan's pilgrims, Hopeful and Christian, deliberated about this sinister counsel. In their wretched and despondent condition, the grave appeared better than prison. Death was more welcome than their present dreadful state. Be that as it may, Hopeful's encouragement to "be patient and endure a while"[2] kept these captives from carrying out the dastardly deed. Then one day, Christian recalled that in his pocket he had the Key of Promise—a key that was sure to open every lock in Doubting Castle. Christian took out the key, unlocked the cell doors, and thrust open the castle gate. At last, they were free from the clutches of Giant Despair!

The pilgrims in this story resisted the temptation to do away with themselves. Yet, many do not endure the taunts of Despair, and they are persuaded to take their own lives. Many of us know friends or

1 John Bunyan, *The Pilgrim's Progress* (Grand Rapids: Revel), 106.
2 John Bunyan, *The Pilgrim's Progress* in the Allegory of a Dream (Wheaton, Illinois: Tyndale House), 142.

family members who have committed suicide. Five times I have received the dreadful news that someone in my family took their own life: step-father, mother, step-brother, brother, and cousin—one gunshot to the head, two asphyxiations, one drug overdose, and one hanging. These loved ones all lost hope and acted upon Despair's urgings. He had triumphed over them from the depths of his miserable dungeon.

Biblical Accounts of Suicide

Suicide is an age-old mode of death; people have been killing themselves for years. Scripture records six suicides[3] (and one attempted suicide[4]), which span both Old Testament and New Testament times: 1) Samson, 2) Saul, 3) Saul's armor bearer, 4) Ahithophel, 5) Zimri, and 6) Judas Iscariot.

Suicide is an age-old mode of death; people have been killing themselves for years.

This list is not mere words on paper. These are names of *actual* people—those who lived in community with others. They were once newborn babies who grew from childhood into young men, and then adults. Some of these men were husbands who left behind grieving wives. Others were fathers, whose children were devastated by their loss. Undoubtedly, each of these men had family members and friends who mourned and grieved their deaths and the tragic way in which they died. Let's briefly examine the stories of these six people.

Samson was born to Manoah and his wife after years of her barrenness (Judges 13:1-2). An angel appeared to Samson's mother

3 Some people count Abimelech's death (Judges 9) as a seventh suicide in the Bible, but actually his death was by the hands of others. When Abimelech was in battle, a woman dropped a millstone on him and crushed his skull. Rather than die by the hands of a woman, Abimelech asked his armor bearer to kill him. Thus, the young man "thrust him through" and he died (Judges 9:54). Since the armor bearer killed Abimelech, his death should not be classified as a suicide.
4 The Philippian jailer in Acts 16:25-34.

to announce his conception and give instructions for his upbringing. Samson became a Nazirite judge of Israel and was a man of incredible strength. However, he was taken prisoner by the Philistines after he succumbed to Delilah's craftiness and his strength left him (Judges 16:5-21). In captivity, Samson was beckoned to entertain the locals at the feast to their god Dagon. It was at this feast that Samson leaned on the supporting pillars of their temple, prayed to God for strength, and said, "Let me die with the Philistines!" Samson "pushed with all his might, and the temple fell on the lords and all the people who were in it," killing himself as well (Judges 16:23-31). Samson's suicide was an act of vengeance on his enemies as well as a release from his horrific suffering in captivity.

Saul, the son of Kish, was appointed Israel's first king. He was a "choice and handsome young man" (1 Samuel 9:2). Saul was married to Ahinoam and had at least five children: three sons (Jonathan, Jishui, and Malchishua), and two daughters (Merab and Michal) (1 Samuel 14:49-50). When Saul was at war with the Philistines, he was severely wounded by archers. Rather than risk torture and final death at the hand of the Philistines, Saul asked his armor bearer to kill him with the sword. The armor bearer was greatly afraid and refused to do so. Therefore Saul took a sword and fell upon it, killing himself (1 Samuel 31:1-5).

We don't know much about *Saul's armor bearer*, but he too killed himself. This armor bearer was likely a young, but strong man appointed by Saul.[5] After watching his king fall on a sword and die, the armor bearer "also fell on his sword, and died with him" (1 Samuel 31:5). His suicide was likely motivated by similar fears to Saul's—that he would be captured, tortured, and killed by the Philistines.

Ahithophel, from the town of Giloh, was a friend and counselor to King David (2 Samuel 15:12). This comrade was known for his wise guidance and advice "as if one had inquired at the oracle of God"

5 See 1 Samuel 14:6, 16:21, and Judges 9:54.

(2 Samuel 16:32). When David fled Jerusalem, Ahithophel betrayed him and joined the insurrection of David's son, Absalom. Ahithophel then became Absalom's adviser. However, when Absalom neglected Ahithophel's recommendations, the men of Israel proclaimed that "the counsel of Hushai the Archite is better than the counsel of Ahithophel" (2 Samuel 17:14). Therefore, when Ahithophel "saw that his counsel was not followed, he saddled his donkey, and arose and went home to his house, to his city. Then he put his household in order, and hanged himself, and died; and he was buried in his father's tomb" (2 Samuel 17:23). It is difficult to know for certain what motivated Ahithophel to hang himself. Perhaps public dishonor and humiliation moved him, or it could have been fear and anxiety that David would execute him for his treachery.

Zimri was the servant of King Elah of Israel, in command of half his chariots (1 Kings 16:8). When King Elah got drunk, Zimri conspired against him, killed him, and proclaimed *himself* king of Israel. Zimri proceeded to slay all the household (including both kinsman and friends) of Elah's father, Baasha. Seven days after Zimri proclaimed himself king, the people of Israel conspired against him and besieged the city of Tirzah where he dwelt. When Zimri saw the city was taken "he went into the citadel of the king's house and burned the king's house down upon himself with fire and died" (1 Kings 16:18). Again, we can't be certain of the motive for his death, but Zimri's suicide was possibly prompted by fear of punishment and execution for his actions.

Judas Iscariot, the son of Simon, is likely the most notorious person to ever commit suicide. Judas was numbered among the twelve handpicked disciples of Jesus—appointed to be with Christ during His earthly ministry (Mark 3:14-19). Judas betrayed his friend and teacher by delivering Him into the hands of His enemies, the chief priests. In return for this betrayal Judas received thirty silver pieces of silver. When he realized the religious leaders intended to kill Jesus, Judas was "remorseful" and returned the silver (Matthew 27:3). He said he had sinned, but it was too late. Then, Judas "departed, and went and hanged himself" (Matthew 27:5). It seems that Judas' guilt and regret was the reason he took his own life.

Today our loved ones commit suicide in response to some of the same circumstances as people in Bible times. Individuals kill themselves as a means of vengeance on enemies. They end their lives in order to escape undesirable situations, impending consequences, or foreseeable suffering. Fear and anxiety is a madness that often incites suicide. Sometimes guilt, regret, dishonor, and humiliation cause people to take their own lives.

No matter the circumstance or method of a loved one's suicide, the pain and suffering experienced by those left behind can be immense.

Other conditions in which our loved ones respond by killing themselves may include: extreme sorrow, depression, loneliness, a terminal diagnosis, or major life changes such as death, divorce, or bankruptcy.

No matter the circumstance or method of a loved one's suicide, the pain and suffering experienced by those left behind can be immense. Shock. Anger. Unanswered questions. Confusion. Shame. Guilt. The list goes on. We lose friends and family members through other means of death such as illness and old age, but grieving a suicide is a *unique sorrow*. It is a loss like no other.

CHAPTER TWO
MOVING FORWARD

How can we go on when someone we know takes their own life? How do we move forward now that "it's over"? My reaction to each suicide was different. The variations were a result of my age, my relationship to (and with) the person, and of course my own relationship with the Lord. By far, the most difficult suffering was when my mother and my brother committed suicide.

I was only 13 years old when my father broke the news that my mother had asphyxiated herself in her garage. My parents were divorced and my mother lived in another town and had remarried. I hadn't seen her for a couple of months. Sadly, our last conversation was about six weeks previous when she called to tell me that her husband had shot himself and was dead. Her words accused me for his death because I had previously spoken against him for threating to kill my father. The next thing I knew my mother was dead by her own hands. She was only 34 years old.

> This childhood nightmare seemed distant and surreal, yet it was ever-present and gut-wrenching

This childhood nightmare seemed distant and surreal, yet it was ever-present and gut-wrenching. I was plagued by confusion, unanswered questions, and overwhelming sorrow. I struggled with intense anger, guilt, and shame. I was livid at what she had done, but then I felt guilty for being mad. I was defensive when others mentioned her death, and I was angry when people said nothing. I felt guilty for past wrongs and blamed myself. I was ashamed and feared what others would think. It was as if I wore a sign that broadcast to the world: "My mother committed suicide!"

> The nightmare grew darker through my own rebellious choices.

The nightmare grew darker through my own rebellious choices. I started getting drunk at parties with my older siblings and their friends. I cut classes, blew off my schoolwork, and my grades plummeted. I was openly defiant and disrespectful to my father, my teachers, and others in authority over me. At the young age of 13, I was on the fast track to ruining my life.

My response to my mother's death shouldn't be surprising—anger, fear, bitterness, despair, selfishness, and pride. In fact, these sins came quite naturally! I had no reason to act any differently. You see, at that time, I didn't have a relationship with Jesus Christ. I didn't know His love, His forgiveness, or His care for me. Sure, I acknowledged there was a God, but I was completely unaware that I was created by Him for a specific purpose, which is to glorify Him.

Life began to change when I turned 15 years old. It was at this time that I attended a Bible camp and heard the words of hope that would ultimately heal my aggrieved heart.

At this camp, I heard from the Bible that "all have sinned and fall short of the glory of God" (Romans 3:23). To *sin* means to miss a mark or a target, or to come up short. I certainly knew that I was a sinner—that I had missed the mark of *something*. The target I had missed was the person of God. My sins of anger, fear of man, bitterness, and more, offended God because these sins are off target from the excellence of who He is. God is wise, righteous, good, kind, merciful, loving, and more, but these attributes are not what characterized me. Nor do these attributes characterize any of mankind—for *all* have sinned and fall short of God's glorious character and attributes.

I also learned from the Bible that mankind's sin against God earns us eternal death and punishment separated from Him. Romans 6:23

says, the "wages of sin is death." There is nothing mankind can do about sin and its consequences. No amount of good things we may say or do will change the fact that we have offended the holy and righteous God who created us to glorify Him.

But I discovered that God has a plan for sin and its consequences. His amazing solution grants *total* forgiveness of our sins, a *complete* release from sin's eternal consequences, and a *thorough* transformation of our hearts. Incredibly, God's plan was for Jesus, God's Son, to become a human. Born as an infant, Jesus was fully God and fully human. He grew into a man and never sinned against God.

As part of God's plan, Jesus was hung on a cross and it was there that God punished Him for all the sins of mankind. Although Jesus was completely sinless, the Bible says that He "bore our sins in His own body on the tree" (1 Peter 2:24). Three days after dying on the cross, Jesus came back to life. He had defeated sin and death by His obedient life, His excruciating suffering, and His glorious resurrection.

His amazing solution grants *total* forgiveness of our sins, a *complete* release from sin's eternal consequences, and a *thorough* transformation of our hearts.

The Bible says that "if you confess with your mouth the Lord Jesus and believe in your heart that God has raised Him from the dead, you will be saved" from your sin (Romans 10:9). For "with the heart one believes to righteousness, and with the mouth confession is made to salvation . . . for whoever calls upon the name of the LORD shall be saved" (Romans 10:10, 13).

I was so relieved to hear these truths and know that Jesus could forgive my sin against God. That day, I spoke a simple prayer to Jesus, confessing my sin and asking forgiveness through His shed blood on the cross.

Accepting Christ's forgiveness of my sin didn't change what had already happened in my life, but it did change my perspective on these circumstances. With a new and redeemed heart, indwelt by the Holy Spirit, I could begin to move forward. I started sorting through the questions and confusion of my mother's death and my own sinful response. It was a process that would last many years as I learned more about God from the Bible.

Accepting Christ's forgiveness of my sin didn't change what had already happened in my life, but it did change my perspective on these circumstances.

I began to work through my sinful anger and bitterness toward my mother. What she had done was wrong and I needed to forgive her: "forgiving one another . . . even as Christ forgave you, so you also must do" (Colossians 3:13). Forgiving someone who is dead sounds strange and impossible, but it isn't. Forgiveness is a deliberate choice that changes your own heart, even if sometimes it can't be translated to others. And so, in obedience to God, I remember verbally expressing that I forgave her for the pain she caused. I deliberately put off my sinful response toward her. Although I knew she couldn't hear me, it didn't matter. I was finally free from the intense anger and bitterness I was harboring toward her.

Another response I needed to work through was the guilt, thinking I had caused my mother's death. Blaming thoughts incessantly plagued me: *If I had been a more obedient little girl she wouldn't have killed herself*, and *I should have put my clean clothes away and turned my socks right-side out*, and *If only I would have said* _____ , or *If only I wouldn't have said* _____ . The accusatory judgments waged on. It was easy to fault myself for her death. Thankfully I realized my perspective was incorrect. I did not cause my mother's death. Every person must "give account of himself to God" (Romans 14:12). Our choices belong to ourselves. My mother made her own decision; it did not belong to me. Certainly, I should confess to God any disobedience and

My mother made her own decision; it did not belong to me.

wrongdoing, but the blame for her death was not mine.

Shame was another heart attitude I needed to sort through. I was overcome by fear of man in which I was overly concerned with what others thought of me. Fear of man is the anxiety of being rejected. It is a self-centered pride which robs the glory that is God's alone. This fear began to dissipate in my mid-twenties when I became a speaker for a national organization. As I shared my life's story, I realized that people didn't judge or condemn me for my mom's choice. Instead, people expressed their love and care for me because of the hurt I had been through. This encouraged me to put off my shameful fear of man.

My hurting heart was beginning to heal as I embraced God's perspective, but I still had the unanswered questions and confusion to sort through. As I grew in my knowledge of God through studying the Bible, I discovered one facet of His character that gave anchor to my soul: God is sovereign. God's sovereignty means that He rules the entire universe. His perfect plans and purposes are always accomplished and can never be thwarted by anyone or anything, including evil. Psalm 33:11 says, "The counsel of the LORD stands forever, the plans of His heart to all generations." God's sovereign rule is not arbitrary, but is always consistent with His other attributes, such as His wisdom, kindness, love, and mercy.

In light of learning about God's sovereignty, I pondered His purposes. I wondered why I had to go through that suffering. I questioned why her intentional death was part of His plan for my life. Clearly, I saw how God used my life's story to encourage and help others, but that didn't appear reason enough. Quite frankly, I thought I would have been better off *with* a mother than *without* one. Certainly, a young daughter needs her mother. And a grown daughter wants a mom to be part of her life as well.

But, God's sovereign rule is always good. His very nature and essence are entirely good. He never does wrong, nor does He mistreat His creation through evil or injustice. "Oh how great is Your goodness, which You have laid up for those who fear You..." (Psalm 31:19a). I may not understand God's plans and purposes for my life, but I can always trust His goodness toward me.

> I may not understand God's plans and purposes for my life, but I can always trust His goodness toward me.

I now know that my greatest need is not for my mother to be alive or to be free from pain and suffering. My greatest need, my *only true* need, is being saved from my sin. God used my mother's suicide and my subsequent rebellion as a catalyst to bring about my salvation.

Not Again!

My step-dad's and mother's suicides were just the beginning. When I was 22, my step-brother asphyxiated himself. When I was 33, my brother overdosed. Just seven months after that, my 14 year-old cousin hung herself. Giant Despair had triumphed over these loved ones. His monstrous advice to "drink this poison" was heeded from the depths of their hopelessness.

Each of these subsequent deaths was hard, but my brother's death was especially difficult. Tony was my only biological brother. He was six years younger than me, and we looked a lot alike. Dark hair, dark eyes, and our smile. As his older sister, I had a motherly sense of protection for him.

Very sadly, Tony and his wife, Jennifer, lost an infant son because of a rare and fatal syndrome called *hydrops fetalis*. Their loss, of course, was devastating. Tony turned to cocaine to comfort his aching soul. Within half a year their marriage was on the verge of collapse. Then came the dreaded one-year anniversary of sweet baby Preston's death. Six days later, Tony was high on cocaine when he swallowed enough prescription opioids and benzodiazepines to lose consciousness and then aspirate his vomit. Lack of oxygen caused his brain to swell and finally a massive cerebral hemorrhage. Tony died the next day.

As a side note, I should mention that my brother's death was officially ruled an accident due to the fact that he aspirated. Some of my family members believe he committed suicide, and others think he overdosed unintentionally; there is evidence for either conclusion. Only God knows the reason Tony ingested those drugs, but this underscores the fact that pain and despair are leading more and more people to abuse both prescription and illegal drugs. Sadly, our loved ones turn to pills and potions to escape life's hardships and they sink deeper into a pit of self-destruction which, far too often, causes death. Current statistics show that over 140 people die *each day* from opioid overdose alone.[6] (In fact, opioid addiction has been declared a national emergency in America.) Regardless if the overdose was intentional or accidental, loved ones are left behind to deal with the tragedy, and many are forced to wrestle with it in the same way as a suicide.

I knew I must bring the darkness of Tony's death to the light of God's Word and see it from His perspective.

When I heard about Tony's overdose, I immediately exhorted myself to humbly accept God's sovereign dealings as good. But, my very next thought was, *this isn't fair!* And the battle ensued. Wrestling with myself over the next few months was intense. I knew I must bring the darkness of Tony's death to the light of God's Word and see it from His perspective. Anything less than God's perspective on my situation would be like a

It is easy to listen to the smorgasbord of the deceiver's lies when you are physically and emotionally exhausted from the shock and grief of a loved one's suicide.

6 http://nypost.com/2017/08/10/trump-declares-opioid-addiction-crisis-a-national-emergency/ and http://nypost.com/2017/08/08/trump-we-have-no-alternative-to-defeating-opioid-crisis/

Band-Aid® on an amputated limb. I already knew from experience the smorgasbord of lies that Satan serves up when someone commits suicide. He lies about the person and character of God, about the Word of God, about your hope and your future, your responsibility in the situation, where to go for help and counsel, and what you really need. Because this deceiver delights in more destruction in the midst of destruction, I knew I must be ready to fight his lies with the truth of God's Word. The aftermath of suicide is a battle that must be fought with God's sword of the Spirit, His Word, if you are to stand against the schemes of the devil (see Ephesians 6:10-18).

CHAPTER THREE

A SMORGASBORD OF LIES AND THE TRUTH OF GOD'S WORD

It is easy to listen to the smorgasbord of the deceiver's lies when you are physically and emotionally exhausted from the shock and grief of a loved one's suicide. Despite this fatigue, you can still take up the weapon of God's Word to fight the lies with His truth. God will give you the spiritual strength to battle as you actively take up the sword of His Word. Your grief is extremely painful, and it will take time to heal, but as you replace the lies with His truth, you will find comfort and hope.

Let's look at some of the lies we are tempted to believe in a suicide situation. I've personally believed some of these lies. A few were passing thoughts that I quickly dismissed as lies, but I struggled with others for a long time. Some are common to people that have lost loved ones to suicide. I haven't listed all the lies one could believe after a suicide, because it seems Satan's smorgasbord comes in all flavors and varieties—each seasoned to our own circumstance. You may discover that you believe a slight variation of the lie I have listed, so don't let the details distract you. The idea is to evaluate whether or not you are taking in the truth of God's Word or if you are dining upon the delicacies of the deceiver's fare.

LIE: My loved one's suicide is my fault.

This is likely the most common lie believed by those who lose a loved one to suicide. There is a strong tendency to blame ourselves. Our prevailing thoughts begin with: *I should have . . . , if only . . ., what if . . . ?* We regret things we didn't do and we regret things we did. Because I fought this lie for so many years in relation to my mother's death, I was prepared to battle it when my brother died. I did have thoughts like: *If only I would have made that phone call; I had planned to do so, or If only he would have received the card I sent days before.* Although the blaming thoughts emerged, I refused to ingest this falsehood. There was nothing I could do or fail to do that would make me responsible for my brother's choice to end his life. When the lies came I had to keep telling myself the truth: Tony was responsible for his choice, not me.

> There is a strong tendency to blame ourselves.

TRUTH: Each person bears the responsibility for his or her own choices.

When Adam and Eve sinned in the Garden of Eden, God judiciously pronounced consequences to each one for their choice (Genesis 3:1-24). Both Adam and Eve opted to eat the fruit of the tree of the knowledge of good and evil, despite the fact God had previously instructed them not to. In God's perfect judgment He did not accept Eve's blame-shifting excuse, "The serpent deceived me and I ate." Rather, He showed Eve that she alone bore the responsibility and the consequences of her own choice. Likewise, God did not accept Adam's defense: "The woman whom You gave to be with me, she gave me of the tree and I ate." Again, in perfect justice, God showed Adam that he alone bore both the responsibility and consequences of his own decision.

> Each of us is responsible for our own choices and not for the choices of another.

This biblical account illustrates the fact that our choices, good or bad, belong to us and no one else. The New Testament echoes this point when it says, "So then each of us shall give account of himself to God" (Romans 14:12). Each of us is responsible for our own choices and not for the choices of another. The only time in history God made someone else bear the responsibility of others' choices was when He charged Jesus with the sin of all mankind and punished Him for that sin on the cross.

As you struggle with this lie, you may argue that you are perhaps guilty of mistreating or sinning against your deceased loved one. Maybe you were in an argument with your loved one before he or she died. Possibly you weren't even on speaking terms when the death occurred. You should know that even if you blatantly sinned against this person, causing a raging fury that provoked the choice to commit suicide, you are still *not* responsible for their death. You are only responsible for someone's death if you pulled the trigger, washed the pills down their throat, or brought about their death in another deliberate way. You may be responsible for sinning against your loved one, but you are not responsible for their death.

If you did sin against your deceased loved one, there is only one thing you can do about it now. You can confess your sin to God, asking His forgiveness through the cleansing blood of Jesus Christ. When you ask His forgiveness, He is a faithful and just God to forgive your sins and cleanse you from all unrighteousness (1 John 1:9).

Don't feast upon the lie that your loved one's suicide is your fault.

Don't feast upon the lie that your loved one's suicide is your fault. The truth is that each person bears the responsibility for his or her own choices. Please consider these verses from God's Word:

> **Say to the righteous that it shall be well with them, for they shall eat the fruit of their doings. Woe to the wicked! It shall be ill with him, for the reward of his hands shall be given him.**
> (Isaiah 3:10-11)

> **The righteousness of the righteous shall be upon himself, and the wickedness of the wicked shall be upon himself.** (Ezekiel 18:20)
>
> **So then each of us shall give account of himself to God**. (Romans 14:12)
>
> **For each one shall bear his own load.** (Galatians 6:5)

LIE: This is more pain than I can take.

I knew it was a big fat lie the second it was out of my mouth. I had thrown myself on the bed and exclaimed that this was more pain than I could take. Seven days after Tony died I miscarried a baby in early pregnancy and I found myself believing the lie that God had given me more suffering than I could bear. The suicide was already more than enough, but now my baby was dead, too.

TRUTH: God comforts our pain and does not push us beyond our ability to obey Him.

After I blurted out my big fat lie, my loving husband responded gently, but firmly, saying, "Julie, get your eyes off yourself." Now, that response may sound harsh to some, but my husband was showing love by speaking the truth to me. He didn't want me believing or speaking lies about God or my circumstances. You see, Ray wanted to remind me of the truth that God does not give us more than we can bear. When we have our eyes fixed upon ourselves, circumstances seem more than we can stand. Then, we are susceptible to wander toward Doubting Castle, leaving us vulnerable to the Giant's taunting.

> When we have our eyes fixed upon ourselves, circumstances seem more than we can stand.

We receive comfort to endure and obey Jesus when we fix our eyes upon Him, despite the most painful of circumstances.

God has never promised a pain-free, trouble-free life. In fact, Jesus said the opposite is true, "In the world you will have tribulation [trouble]" (John 16:33). But God will be with us in our distress: "Yea, though I walk through the valley of the shadow of death, I will fear no evil; for You are with me" (Psalm 23:4; see also Matthew 28:20b). One of my greatest comforts as I grieved the simultaneous loss of my brother and my baby was knowing that God was with me. The valley was still dark and I had to walk through it, but I was comforted with His presence.

We receive comfort to endure and obey Jesus when we fix our eyes upon Him, despite the most painful of circumstances. Basically, we have two choices in our suffering: 1) believe the lie that it is too much, focusing on our pain and ourselves, or 2) believe the truth that God does not overburden us, fixing our eyes upon Jesus in our pain. Please consider these verses from God's Word:

> **No temptation [trial] has overtaken you except such as is common to man; but God is faithful, who will not allow you to be tempted [tested] beyond what you are able, but with the temptation [testing] will also make the way of escape, that you may be able to bear it.**
> (1 Corinthians 10:13)

> **Therefore we also, since we are surrounded by so great a cloud of witnesses, let us lay aside every weight, and the sin which so easily ensnares us, and let us run with endurance the race that is set before us, looking unto Jesus, the author and finisher of our faith, who for the joy that was set before Him endured the cross, despising the**

> **shame, and has sat down at the right hand of the throne of God. For consider Him who endured such hostility from sinners against Himself, lest you become weary and discouraged in your souls.** (Hebrews 12:1-3)

> **. . . His divine power has given to us all things that pertain to life and godliness, through the knowledge of Him who called us by glory and virtue.** (2 Peter 1:3)

LIE: The Bible doesn't address my situation.

In our day of scientific advancement it's easy to place our trust in social services, psychological counsel, and medical professionals. It is easy to believe that they, rather than God, have all the insight and practical answers to help in difficult situations. Though God has given mankind the discernment and ability for technical progress, it is not meant to replace the all-sufficient wisdom of God's Word—the Bible.

We tend to think the Bible is not adequate because we cannot find in it the modern names of syndromes and sicknesses that befall mankind. God's Word is not viewed as practical for us or family. Consequently, we believe the lie that His Word is not sufficient and we accept the guidance of the world, which often runs contrary to God's counsel. It is a lie to believe that secular wisdom, as practical as it may seem, is adequate or sufficient counsel. Many people embrace this falsehood after a suicide, especially when the situation is extremely complex and convoluted.

TRUTH: God's Word gives sufficient counsel for any situation. God is the Creator and Knower of the human heart. He cares for and loves mankind. Therefore, He has kindly provided His wisdom to navigate life. This wisdom can be found in the Bible.

The Bible contains truths and principles to give us sufficient counsel for any circumstance—even suicide.

The Bible addresses topics such as anthropology, psychology, history, sociology, biology, theology, geology, geography, philosophy, and a host of other "ologys." It is a book about family relationships (both good and bad), death and dying, times of war and times of peace, deception, stealing, cheating, good and evil, hope, comfort, friends and enemies, sin and salvation, the character and plans of God, the person of Jesus Christ, the power of the Holy Spirit, and a host of other subjects.

The Bible contains truths and principles to give us sufficient counsel for any circumstance—even suicide. We only need to approach His Word with humility in order to learn from Him. Please consider these verses from God's Word:

> **Your testimonies also are my delight and my counselors. Unless Your law had been my delight, I would then have perished in my affliction.** (Psalm 119:24, 92)
>
> **Your words were found and I ate them, and Your word was to me the joy and rejoicing of my heart; for I am called by Your name, O LORD God of Hosts.** (Jeremiah 15:16)
>
> **All Scripture is given by inspiration of God and is profitable for doctrine, for reproof, for correction, for instruction in righteousness, that the man of God may be complete, thoroughly equipped for every good work.** (2 Timothy 3:16)

> **For the Word of God is living and powerful, and sharper than any two edged sword, piercing even to the division of soul and spirit and of joints and marrow, and is a discerner of thoughts and intents of the heart.** (Hebrews 4:12)

LIE: God didn't have anything to do with this awful situation.

> We wonder if this situation was outside the realm of God's influence and control.

It's normal to ask, "Where was God when my loved one committed suicide?" Because God is good and kind, some may think He had nothing to do with the evil incident. Perhaps He was on vacation or sleeping when our loved one died. Also, because Satan is wicked and cruel, some think he alone is culpable for the awful situation. Perhaps he usurped God's rule and thwarted His good plans. We wonder if this situation was outside the realm of God's influence and control.

TRUTH: God is sovereign; His plans and purposes are always accomplished.

The Bible teaches that God is sovereign—He rules the entire universe. His perfect plans and purposes are *always* accomplished and can never be thwarted by anyone or anything, including evil. God alone possesses all power (omnipotence) over His creation. He has all knowledge (omniscience) of all things. And, He is present in all places at all times (omnipresent). God's sovereign rule is never arbitrary. It is always consistent with His other attributes, such as His wisdom, His kindness, His love, and His mercy.

God's sovereignty extends over everything He has created: heavenly beings, human beings, all living creatures, and inanimate matter. That means that God and Satan are *not* equal powers vying for control over the universe. Satan and the other demonic beings were created by God and are subject to their Creator. Therefore, Satan can *never* thwart God's sovereign plans. Although Satan seeks to deceive and destroy, he cannot do anything without God's authorization. For example, he had to ask Jesus for permission to "sift" the Apostle Peter as wheat (Luke 22:31). Satan could not even touch Job without God first granting him consent, and even then, he was limited to what God would allow (Job 1:12; 2:5-6).

God had a role in the suicides of my family members. He was not asleep nor did He turn His back on these situations for even a moment. Satan did not usurp the sovereign will of God or thwart His plans in any way. Certainly, God's mandate was for my loved ones to endure their suffering in obedience to Him. Yet, He sovereignly ordained the years of their lives to be what they were (Psalm 139:16). They did not take one more or one less breath than what God had planned for their lives. For "in His hand is the life of every living thing and the breath of all mankind" (Job 12:10).

Satan did not usurp the sovereign will of God or thwart His plans in any way.

If God is sovereign, did He kill my loved ones? No. Each of these people chose to take their own life. We don't understand how God is sovereign while at the same time each person has responsibility for his or her own choices. It takes faith to believe this truth. In faith we can be assured that God always accomplishes His perfect plans and purposes. Please consider these verses from God's Word:

> **He is unique, and who can make Him change;**
> **And whatever His soul desires, that He does.**
> **For He performs what is appointed for me. . . .**
> (Job 23:13-14a)

> **Then Job answered the LORD and said: "I know that you can do everything, and that no purpose of Yours can be withheld from You."** (Job 42:2)
>
> **The counsel of the LORD stands forever, the plans of His heart from generation to generation.** (Psalm 33:11)
>
> **Ah, LORD God! Behold You have made the heavens and the earth by Your outstretched arm. There is nothing too difficult for You.** (Jeremiah 32:17)
>
> **. . . He does according to His will in the host of heaven and among the inhabitants of earth; and no one can ward off His hand or say to Him, "What have You done?"** (Daniel 4:35)

LIE: God was wrong to let my loved one die.

It's not fair! That was my thought after hearing about my brother's overdose. Even though I had immediately urged myself to humbly accept God's sovereign dealings as good, within twenty-four hours I was telling God how it should have been. Sobbing aloud to Him I said, "This wasn't the way things were supposed to turn out! Tony was my brother, Lord, my only brother! How could you let this happen? Why?" In the weeks following Tony's death I had trouble seeing God's goodness. I thought I knew Him to be a good God, but it didn't look that way in this situation. It appeared He had done wrong.

> I thought I knew Him to be a good God, but it didn't look that way in this situation.

TRUTH: God's supreme rule is always consistent with the beauty of His divine character.

It is human nature to charge God with wrong when things don't go our way. Anger and blaming come from swallowing the lie that God is not good. But He *is* good! God is sovereign over all, and He doesn't rule capriciously. His supreme rule is always consistent with the beauty of His divine character. He is wise, good, righteous, loving, and more. Therefore, He always rules with wisdom, goodness, righteousness, and love—along with His other attributes. In perfect wisdom, God knows the best plans for everyone and everything in every circumstance. He never acts in folly, ignorance, or error. Our finite human understanding may not always see the magnificence of His divine character as He rules, but its beauty is there.

After my brother died, I contemplated the truth of God's sovereign goodness. I trembled when I considered my necessary response—worship. Our God must be praised. *Rejoice in the Lord*, my heart whispered (Philippians 4:4). The firm reply: *But I can't!* And again the whisper: *Rejoice in the Lord.* I wrestled on, knowing that the degree to which I rejoiced in and was satisfied in my God was the degree to which I glorified Him. I desperately wanted to glorify Him. My heart welled-up and I uttered aloud to my King: "Help, Lord! I don't understand. Please, please give me the faith to rejoice in Your sovereign plans and believe You are still good, even though I can't see it." I spoke these words in amazement, hardly believing I could verbalize them. Thanks be to God that, by faith, I was able to embrace His sovereign plans instead of believing lies and charging Him with wrong. I won a significant heart-battle that day as I grieved my brother's death.

> While we live on this earth we will never fully understand God's perfect sovereignty.

While we live on this earth we will never fully understand God's perfect sovereignty. It's a truth too difficult for finite minds.

"For My thoughts are not your thoughts, nor are your ways My ways," says the LORD. "For as the heavens are higher than the earth, so are My ways higher than your ways, and My thoughts than your thoughts." (Isaiah 55:8-9)

We will probably always have questions about God's sovereignty. It's alright to ask, "Why?", but it's best not to camp-out on that question. Through faith, we can quickly answer with the truth that God is sovereign and His supreme rule is *always* good. Please consider these verses from God's Word:

Through faith, we can quickly answer with the truth that God is sovereign and His supreme rule is *always* good.

He is the Rock, His work is perfect; for all His ways are justice, a God of truth and without injustice; righteous and upright is He. (Deuteronomy 32:4)

The LORD is righteous in all His ways, gracious in all His works. (Psalm 145:17)

O LORD, You are my God. I will exalt You, I will praise Your name; for You have done wonderful things; Your counsels of old are faithfulness and truth. (Isaiah 25:1)

Though He causes grief, yet He will show compassion according to the multitude of His mercies. (Lamentations 3:32)

Oh, the depth of the riches both of the wisdom and knowledge of God! How unsearchable are His judgments and His ways past finding out!

> **For who has known the mind of the Lord? Or who has become His counselor?"**
> (Romans 11:33-34)

LIE: Suicide is a genetic trait or a family curse, so there is no hope for my family.

Seven months after Tony died, my 14 year old cousin, Ashley, hung herself with a belt in her closet. The next day, Ashley's mom (my mother's sister) responded in despair by overdosing on prescription pills. Thankfully, immediate medical treatment preserved her life. *What is wrong with this family?* I thought. *This has got to stop!* I was sick and tired of hearing about suicide–especially in my own family!

In the weeks following Ashley's suicide, I became extremely anxious and fearful. My three sons (who were ages five, seven, and nine at that time) had been exposed to the suicides of two family members in less than a year. I worried that our sons might someday heed Giant Despair's urging, choosing to end their lives. I wrestled with God and became angry. Why had He allowed our children to be exposed to such horrible things? Sin was wreaking havoc in my heart because I fed on the lie that my future was doomed due to my family's "tradition" of committing suicide. Fear overwhelmed me and I struggled to think rightly about God and my circumstances.

Their choice to commit suicide was a self-centered act that failed to account for the devastation it would cause others.

TRUTH: Suicide is a sinful choice.

Suicide is not a genetic trait nor is it a family curse. It is a sinful choice. Their choice to commit suicide was a self-centered act that failed to account for the devastation it would cause others. I dearly loved my family members who committed suicide, but what they did was wrong. I don't judge these loved ones for their choice. I have compassion for the pain they suffered, but I sure wish they had chosen differently.

Ashley's suicide note was hastily scribbled in blue crayon. It read, "Sick of hurting." Tony didn't leave a note, but his could have said the same. In fact, all five were truly heartbroken people. They were in great distress of soul and trial of circumstance.

What went wrong that they chose to end their lives? It wasn't genetics and it wasn't a generational curse. It was sin. Although I don't know their hearts, it's likely each of my family members chose to believe the lie that their pain was greater than they could handle and that they deserved better than what God (or "life") had given them. They chose to focus on relieving their own pain, rather than bearing in mind the anguish they would cause surviving loved ones. In this they were prideful to esteem themselves above others.

Sadly, my loved ones didn't see God's sovereign goodness in their circumstances. They chose to lean on their own limited understanding and perspective instead of God's. Even more unfortunate, they put themselves in the place of God—the Holder of Life and Breath—and took life and breath into their own hands.

Many of us get discouraged and despair of life at one time or another. Even men in the Bible, who loved and served God, were despondent due to various circumstances. Great heroes of the faith like Job (Job 3:20-21), Moses (Numbers 11:14-15), Elijah (1 Kings 19:4), and the Apostle Paul (2 Corinthians 1:8) cried out to God in anguish and hopelessness.

> Suicide is just another form of escape—*a permanent one.*

So why do some people endure difficulty while others choose to act upon Despair's taunts from the dungeon? Why do some families, like mine, have a high incidence of suicide? I think there are a couple explanations. First, not all families have members who love and serve God. Many, actually *most* in my family do not have a personal, saving relationship with Jesus Christ. Therefore, sins such as anger, pride, and selfishness are the natural response to conflicts, trials, and hardships, rather than perseverance through faith.

Second, families can have a high incidence of suicide because the natural patterns of sin are modeled in daily living. People often follow examples they see before them, and this is especially true in family dynamics. For example, parents show such actions as fleeing arguments, avoiding people, withdrawing in conflicts, giving the silent treatment, and numbing life's pain through alcohol and drugs. Divorce and separation, job changes, frequent moves, and severed relationships are presented as acceptable methods to deal with life's problems. This sinful escape mentality is on display every day. Suicide is just another form of escape—*a permanent one*.

Although my sons were exposed to the suicides of family members, they are not cursed or genetically wired to do likewise. They have as much of a choice as anyone. Instead of letting pride rule them, they can choose humility. Instead of being selfish, they can choose to esteem others above themselves. Instead of living with anger, they can choose to joyfully accept God's sovereign goodness. Of course, they will probably become discouraged at times, but they are not doomed to follow the Giant's temptation to end their life. Please consider these verses from God's Word:

> **Therefore do not let sin reign in your mortal body, that you should obey it in its desires. And do not present your members as instruments of unrighteousness to sin, but present yourselves to God as being alive from the dead, and your members as instruments of righteousness to God.**
> (Romans 6:12-13)

But God be thanked that though you were slaves of sin, yet you obeyed from the heart that form of doctrine to which you were delivered. And having been set free from sin, you became slaves of righteousness. (Romans 6:17-18)

Therefore, if anyone is in Christ, he is a new creation, old things have passed away; behold all things have become new. (2 Corinthians 5:17)

I say then walk in the Spirit, and you shall not fulfill the desire of the flesh. And those who are Christ's have crucified the flesh with its passions and desires. (Galatians 5:16, 24)

I, therefore, the prisoner of the Lord, exhort you to have a walk worthy of the calling with which you were called. (Ephesians 4:1)

Be renewed in the spirit of your mind, and that you put on the new man which was created according to God, in righteousness and true holiness. (Ephesians 4:23)

LIE: People who commit suicide go to hell.

Some people believe and teach that anyone who commits suicide goes to hell. This opinion may originate from the fact that Jesus called Judas Iscariot "the son of perdition" (John 17:12), which means damnation or destruction. Judas wasn't damned to hell because he killed himself. He was accursed because he betrayed the Son of God, was unrepentant, and was possessed by Satan.

> Some people believe and teach that anyone who commits suicide goes to hell.

In addition to this misguided notion about Judas, there may be other reasons people believe that those who commit suicide go to hell. No matter the explanation for this widespread belief, it is simply a lie.

TRUTH: People who have received Jesus' forgiveness of sin go to be with Him; those who haven't go to hell.

The mode of physical death does not matter—old age or accident, disease or murder, even suicide. A person's eternal destiny is not determined by how they die. A person's everlasting dwelling place is established based on their relationship with Jesus Christ.

> A person's eternal destiny is not determined by how they die.

Although everyone has sinned and fallen short of God's glory (Romans 3:23), God is desirous that people be at peace with Him. He has provided His Son Jesus to bring about this peace: "When we were enemies we were reconciled to God through the death of His Son . . ." (Romans 5:10). God is righteous and just to punish sin, but He is equally merciful and gracious to grant forgiveness to those who ask for it.

> God is righteous and just to punish sin, but He is equally merciful and gracious to grant forgiveness to those who ask for it.

And so, all people everywhere for all of time have fallen into one of two categories. The first category is comprised of those who *do not* have a personal relationship with Jesus Christ because they have not received forgiveness for their sins. The Bible teaches that those who have not received forgiveness of sin will spend eternity in everlasting punishment: ". . . those who do not obey the gospel of our Lord Jesus Christ [will] be punished with everlasting destruction from the presence of the Lord and from the glory of His power" (2 Thessalonians 1:8b-9).

The second category of people is made up of those who *do* have a personal relationship with Jesus Christ because they have received forgiveness for their sin. The Bible declares that those who have received forgiveness will be "raised up together and will sit in the heavenly places in Christ Jesus" (Ephesians 2:6), and they "shall see His face" (Revelation 22:4), and they "shall always be with the Lord" (1 Thessalonians 4:17).

Therefore, in regard to death by suicide, if a person commits suicide and has not received forgiveness of sin, this person will not spend eternity in the presence of the Lord. However, if someone has received forgiveness of sin, and sadly, chooses to commit suicide, this person will still spend eternity in the presence of the Lord. It is tragic and heartbreaking to choose Giant Despair's counsel rather than God's promises, and thus enter Heaven through an unrighteous act. Not only is this sinful deed distressing to those left behind, but the person who died could lose eternal rewards (1 Corinthians 3:13-14), and may even be ashamed before Christ (1 John 2:28) for not enduring in faith—for God has promised to not test us beyond what we are able to bear (1 Corinthians 10:13). Although salvation includes forgiveness of *all* sin—past, present, and future (John 5:24; Colossians 2:13)—suicide should never be the answer to our suffering. Please consider these verses from God's Word:

> **But as many as received Him to them He gave the right to become children of God, to those who believe in His name.** (John 1:12)
>
> **For God so loved the world that He gave His only begotten Son, that whoever believes in Him should not perish but have everlasting life.** (John 3:16)
>
> **He who believes in the Son has everlasting life; and he who does not believe the Son shall not see life, but the wrath of God abides on him.** (John 3:36)

> **Jesus said . . . "I am the way, the truth, and the life. No one comes to the Father except through Me."** (John 14:6)

> **For the wages of sin is death, but the gift of God is eternal life in Christ Jesus our Lord.** (Romans 6:23)

LIE: My loved one's suicide has ruined my life!

> A return to normal life is difficult to imagine.

"There is no recovering from this!" "I am scarred for life!" "This baggage will follow me everywhere!" "Everything is ruined!" It's easy to make statements like these when you experience the devastation of a loved one's suicide. A return to normal life is difficult to imagine. The tears won't cease. The brain fog doesn't clear. The pain won't go away. Oh, and the reminders are everywhere. It seems that life is ruined.

TRUTH: God doesn't waste a hurt; He uses suffering for our good.

Your life is not ruined because of your loved one's suicide. I understand the intense pain, confusion, grief, and heartache caused by the suicide of a loved one. I know that in grappling with this kind of tragedy it is easy to wander toward Giant Despair's Doubting Castle. Soon, we too can find ourselves in the confines of his dark, stinking dungeon. There the giant beats *us* mercilessly. We are weak and vulnerable and he is ruthless and relentless. His counsel remains the same, "Drink this poison, for why should you choose life, seeing it is attended with so much bitterness?" Yet, we do not have to heed Despair's advice because there is hope in Christ. There is life—yes, even a *joyful* life—after the suicide of a loved one.

> God can even take something as horrific as a suicide and use it for good.

God doesn't waste a hurt; He uses suffering for our good. God can even take something as horrific as a suicide and use it for good. In fact, He promises to use *all things* for good in the lives of those who love Him. We are assured of this in the book of Romans, "And we know that all things work together for good to those who love God, to those who are the called according to His purpose. For whom He foreknew, He also predestined to be conformed to the image of His Son . . ." (Romans 8:28-29). The "good" that God works is our becoming more like Jesus—which is His ultimate purpose for those who know Him.

When we remember that God will bring good from our suffering, we can choose to rejoice in it (see James 1:2-4 below). We may not see the good while we are suffering, or even in months and years to come. Yet, we can still walk by faith in God's promise. This faith will help us endure and rejoice despite our suffering. Please consider these truths from God's Word:

> **And not only that, but we also glory in tribulations, knowing that tribulation produces perseverance, and perseverance character, and character hope. Now hope does not disappoint, because the love of God has been poured out in our hearts by the Holy Spirit who was given to us.** (Romans 5:3-5)
>
> **Therefore I take pleasure in infirmities, in reproaches, in needs, in persecutions, in distresses, for Christ's sake. For when I am weak, then I am strong.** (2 Corinthians 12:10)
>
> **Before I was afflicted I went astray, but now I keep Your Word. It is good for me that I have been afflicted that I may learn Your statutes.** (Psalm 119:67, 71)

My brethren, count it all joy when you fall into various trials, knowing that the testing of your faith produces endurance. But let endurance have its perfect work, that you may be mature and complete, lacking nothing. (James 1:2-4)

In this you greatly rejoice, though now for a little while, if need be, you have been grieved by various trials, that the genuineness of your faith, being much more precious than gold that perishes though it is tested by fire, may be found to praise, honor, and glory at the revelation of Jesus Christ. (1 Peter 1:6-7)

But may the God of all grace, who called us to His eternal glory by Christ Jesus, after you have suffered a while, perfect, establish, strengthen, and settle you. To Him be the glory and the dominion forever and ever. Amen.
(1 Peter 5:10-11)

CHAPTER FOUR
FINAL THOUGHTS

My own life is an example of God's amazing power to bring blessing in the midst of chaos. As I have mentioned, it was my mother's suicide that exposed my rebellious heart—which caused me to recognize my sin and need for salvation. Remarkably, in God's sovereign goodness, He used calamity to bring me to a saving knowledge of Jesus Christ.

> Having a personal, saving relationship with Jesus is the starting point to move forward after a loved one's death.

If you have lost someone to suicide, your greatest need is forgiveness of sin through Jesus Christ. If you have not yet received His forgiveness, you can do that right now by talking to Him. You might say something like this:

> *Dear God, I admit to you that I am a sinner. I have missed the mark of Your perfect character. I recognize that I was created in your image and likeness in order to give you glory, but I have fallen short of that glory. Because I am a sinner, I deserve death, which is eternal punishment and separation from you.*
>
> *I ask your forgiveness for my sin, believing you sent Your Son Jesus to suffer the undeserved punishment for sin. He was crucified on a cross and then died. He was buried and then rose again three days later. I believe Jesus is the only way for my sin to be forgiven and to live eternally in your presence.*
>
> *Thank you for forgiving me. Amen.*

Having a personal, saving relationship with Jesus is the starting point to move forward after a loved one's death. Accepting Christ's forgiveness of your sin won't change what has already happened, but it will change your perspective on your situation. With a new and redeemed heart, you can now move forward. As you learn more about God and study the Bible passages in this booklet, He will help you sort through the questions and confusion of your loved one's death and your own response to it. You don't have to be a miserable hostage in the dungeon of Giant Despair's Doubting Castle. God's Word is the "Key" of freedom to unlock the prison doors and bring comfort and healing to your hurting heart.

For those of you who already have a personal relationship with Jesus Christ, I earnestly encourage you to take up your weapons—the sword of truth and the shield of faith (Ephesians 6:16-17). As you do, He will strengthen you to rest upon the truth of His Word, rather than believe the smorgasbord of the devil's lies. The battle to grieve a suicide is intense, but our God comforts and heals.

From my own experience, I can say that our God, the God of all comforts, *will* comfort you in *all* of your suffering. And someday, you will be able to console others with the comfort which you have received from Him (2 Corinthians 1:2). Then together we will say, "Blessed be the God and Father of our Lord Jesus Christ, the Father of mercies and God of all comforts" (2 Corinthians 1:3).